The Xenophobe's® Guide to The Danes

Helen Dyrbye
Steven Harris
Thomas Golzen

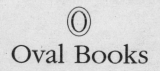

Oval Books

Published by Oval Books
335 Kennington Road
London SE11 4QE
United Kingdom

Telephone: +44 (0)20 7582 7123
Fax: +44 (0)20 7582 1022
E-mail: info@ovalbooks.com
Web site: www.ovalbooks.com

First published by Ravette Publishing, 1997
First published by Oval Books, 1999
Updated 2000, 2001, 2002
Reprinted 2004

Editor – Catriona Tulloch Scott
Series Editor – Anne Tauté

Cover designer – Jim Wire, Quantum
Printer – Cox & Wyman Ltd.
Producer – Oval Projects Ltd.

Distributed in Denmark by Forlaget Buster
Telephone: +45 39 69 2100
E-mail: pilegard@inet.uni2.dk

Xenophobe's® is a Registered Trademark.

Cover: Thanks are given to the LEGO Group for
the use of their bricks. LEGO and LEGO brick
are Trademarks of the LEGO Group.

ISBN-13: 978-1-902825-24-1
ISBN-10: 1-902825-24-1

Contents

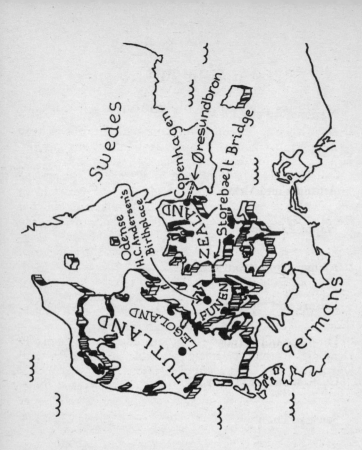

The Danish population is 5.4 million, compared with 9 million Swedes who like Denmark for duty-free beer, and 82 million Germans who like Denmark for sun, sand and sea holidays.

Denmark is made up of 406 islands. It is a little larger than The Netherlands and could fit into Sweden ten times (and has tried at various times in history). The state of Denmark includes Greenland which is nearly four times the size of France, which is not much use since 95% of it happens to be covered in ice.

Apart from Copenhagen, no town has over 250,000 inhabitants and few have more than 50,000, unless the weather is very sunny and the Swedes very thirsty.

Nationalism and Identity

The Danes and Their Neighbours

Denmark is a Scandinavian country, but not a very Scandinavian country. It has no midnight sun, no ski-jumps and no reindeer.

Outsiders tend to think that all Scandinavians are the same, but they are not. The Swedes are the Prussians of the North; they stand up straight, dress alike and do what they are told. The Norwegians are like the Scots; a hardy mountain folk. The Danes are more relaxed and easy-going. They tend to sit down: it increases the chances of everyone seeing eye to eye.

The differences between these three peoples are best understood by considering the most famous writer of each country: Hans Christian Andersen for Denmark, Ibsen for Norway, and Strindberg for Sweden.

They are also reflected in attitudes to alcohol. In Denmark alcohol is freely available. In Norway and Sweden alcohol sales are under state control; a licence is needed not just to sell alcohol, but to buy it. Yet, if someone is noisily drunk in Copenhagen, just across the water from Sweden, there is a better than even chance that the drunk is a Swedish export. No Swedish politician would ever be seen with a beer in his hand, but a Danish politician would be happy not only to have a beer in his hand, but to be seen drinking it.

The Danes think of their neighbours as they would members of their family. The other Scandinavian countries are of course brothers. Norway is accepted as equal, perhaps even slightly admired for its natural beauty and exclusivity. Sweden is the boring older brother who thinks he knows best. The Finns are moody, unpredictable and possibly autistic. Germany is the indulgent uncle, patting heads with disconcerting shows of affection.

The Swedish countryside is much admired and many

Danes holiday in Sweden, but they feel somehow that Swedes don't deserve their wonderful surroundings. Sweden in Danish eyes is a cultural and human desert. Taxes are extortionate, there are rules about everything and a beer costs about £5 ($8) in a café. Both countries have fines for dogs fouling the pavement, but in Sweden you actually get caught.

In the spirit of New Europe, Danes try very hard to like the Germans, but it's hard work. They are convinced that the Germans are trying to take over Europe, cunningly disguised as tourists. They are intensely concerned that the *pølse tyskere* (sausage Germans) will buy Jutland as soon as they get the chance and turn it into a windsurfing centre. Germans regularly fall asleep on their sailboards and have to be fished out of the North Sea halfway to Grimsby by the long-suffering Danish air-sea rescue service. All the summer houses are rented out to Germans, there are even German editions of local newspapers, and LEGOLAND, complete with a part of the Rhein Valley, is filled to the brim with Germans determined to enjoy themselves.

Germans are more acceptable if they buy plenty of Danish products. They are also partially forgiven for being German if they employ Danes in their businesses.

Inflation in Denmark is negligible, the economy is strong and technical development is world-class – not bad for a country with a population roughly that of South London. The Danes attribute this success to their having all the virtues of their neighbours and none of their vices. They share the Germans' methodical attention to detail and the Swedes' egalitarianism and level-headedness. Gone is the plodding, constipated German imagination (or lack of it) and the dreary Swedish party-pooping pedantry. According to the Danes, what's left is a unique mixture of conscientiousness and informality which makes the Danish overseas traveller breathe a sigh of relief when he crosses the border home.

High Fliers

The Danes fly their flag with pride. The red and white 'Dannebrog' against a clear blue sky is enough to bring a tear to their eyes. Rural inhabitants invariably have their own flag pole set squarely in the middle of their garden. Town dwellers rent an allotment and plant a pole along with their broad-leaved parsley. Both have lists of dates magneted to the fridge giving details of when to 'let rip' – public holidays, festivals, state visits, their own birthdays, anniversaries, etc., and town 'fêtes'. Twice a month each town lines its main street with flags to remind everyone that the local shops stay open late that Saturday.

Danes who cannot fly flags out of doors have mini flagpoles as part of their table decoration for high days and holidays, and they even fly the flag from the food on cocktail-sticks. Shops and advertisers use the flag to promote their goods, and Danish football fans were the first to paint their faces with their national flag.

There is nothing threatening about this nationalism. As a nation, the Danes have not been a threat to anyone for hundreds of years.

How They See Others

The rugged individualism of American society is at odds with the importance which Danes attach to social cohesion. Americans are seen as useful allies and the scientific research they generate is admired, but if a situation is approaching unacceptable levels, for example, Danish children are being fed too much fast food, a Danish academic of some description will appear on the news proclaiming that Denmark is hurtling towards an 'amerikansk tilstand' (an American state of affairs).

The British are regarded as class-ridden with Dickensian social values, a view supported by costume dramas shown

7

on television. This does not prevent Danes from showing great enthusiasm for English pop music and league football. Though deeply censorious of the Germans and pitying of the Swedes, the Danes are angels of patience and tolerance when it comes to the English. The drunken buffoonery of the English football fans is met with smiles of understanding. The sight of an Arsenal fan halfway up a lamp-post swilling beer from the anus of an inflatable rubber pig caused little more than some shaking of heads. A German or a Swede would have been arrested and heavily fined.

The Danes look on the outside world confident that they may not have achieved a perfect society, but they have got closer to it than most other people. There are really only two things that Danes may envy other nations: one is warm winters, and the other is a beautiful language.

How They See Themselves

Efficient, environmentally conscious and generous to those less fortunate are the kind of words most Danes would use to describe themselves and their society today. However, behind this idyllic description lurks the Danish tax man, '*skattefar*' (tax daddy), wielding more power than George Orwell's Big Brother.

The substantial taxes needed to support the well-developed welfare system (about 50%) seem to be chalking up an ever-widening distinction between those who work and those who don't. Scratch the surface and you find that the Danes' image of themselves varies a great deal.

At one extreme there are self-employed Danes who see themselves as freedom fighters. For them, hours of extra paperwork mean that a working day often stretches into the night, and 'black work' (moonlighting) is a national sport. At the other extreme, a number of Danes languishing on one of the highest unemployment benefits in Europe are willing to fail compulsory job interviews to let fellow citizens have the jobs that are available.

The majority of the population happily jogs along on the verge of Utopia, somewhere between the two.

Danes think that being Danish is a privilege and makes them special. They say that if Scandinavia is a bowl of rice pudding, Denmark is the '*smørhul*' – the golden hollow in the middle, full of melted butter.

The Danes' mission in life is to help the rest of the world to see just how wonderful Denmark is. They feel sorry for all the poor souls who aren't Danish, have never visited their country, or otherwise live in heathen ignorance of their land of milk and honey. However, they cannot bring themselves to boast about how fantastically talented they are so they use an inordinate amount of time and energy trying to get others to see the light.

How They See Other Danes

Even within such a small country as Denmark there are strong regional differences. Copenhageners make great show of not being able to understand some of the thicker regional accents in Jutland and regard travelling there with foreboding. Jutlanders are seen as rural masters of understatement. According to popular belief, the Jutlander rarely says anything downright positive, e.g., when asked if he wants coffee, he doesn't say "Yes", he says "I wouldn't say no." Jutlanders see Copenhageners as slick, silver-tongued city-dwellers who do them an injustice. They claim they are "not as bad" as all that.

In fact, all Danes have a better opinion of themselves than they allow themselves to express.

How Others See Them

The Danes are seen as the epitome of good order and good sense. They are not very excitable or romantic, they have neat painted houses set in neat countryside and wear sensible shoes – a bit like the Swiss, but without the mountains.

Their language is unlearnable, their cultural identity elusive, but everybody likes the Danes. It is impossible not to like the creators of LEGO, the producers of so much bacon and butter, and the brewers of (probably) the best beer in the world.

Character

Today's Danes are a peaceable people. The only helmeted warriors left are bikers. When the Danish Vikings colonised the British Isles, they must have taken with them all the most unruly elements. Ever since, the British have behaved like Vikings, while the Danes have constructed a modern liberal welfare state where everyone is cared for, and their football fans are models of propriety.

Denmark is a land of modesty and moderation. This is largely a consequence of the Danes' sense of social responsibility. The touchstone of any activity or point of view is whether it is *samfundsrelevant*, that is, socially useful.

Indoctrination concerning the individual's responsibility begins early. Danish children are brought up with stories which feature Teddy, Chicken and Duckling. Teddy and his friends regularly face the conflict of individual needs versus the common good. The peak-rated televised version shows the characters having a witty and wonderful time, eating, drinking, dancing and laughing, so the young get the idea that social responsibility does not have to be onerous. Adults are still enchanted, not so much by the message as by the sight of three grown-ups wearing fur costumes, huffing and puffing about in a forest while trying to sing and avoid heatstroke in unison.

However, to really get to grips with the Danish character one needs to understand two words: *hygge* and *Janteloven*.

Hygge

A love of or need for *hygge* is an important part of the Danish psyche. *Hygge* is usually inadequately translated as 'cosiness'. This is too simplistic: cosiness relates to physical surroundings – a jersey can be cosy, or a warm bed – whereas *hygge* has more to do with people's behaviour towards each other. It is the art of creating intimacy: a sense of comradeship, conviviality, and contentment rolled into one.

Friends meeting in the street might say that it has been *hyggeligt* to see each other, and someone who is fun to be with can be called a *hyggelig fyr*, when he would hardly be described as a 'cosy fellow'. The truly emotive depth of the word *hyggelig* is best captured by considering its opposite, *uhyggeligt*, which means anything from cheerless through sinister to downright shocking and grisly.

To have a *hyggelig* time is social nirvana in Denmark. Candlelight is used to encourage a *hyggelig* atmosphere. In fact, the Danes are mad about candles and use them everywhere, both in public places like cafés, bars and restaurants, and in the home. The dim lighting helps to soften the clean, uncluttered surfaces and uncompromising white walls that are typical features of Danish living rooms. Everyone's ideal is to have a Christiania *kakkelovn* (antique stove) or an open fireplace and feel the warmth from its *hyggelige* glow.

Achieving *hygge* generally involves being with friends and family, and eating and drinking. Older Danes are

11

horrified to hear of youngsters who *hygger* themselves alone on the sofa with a rented video and family-size bag of sweets.

Janteloven

Whenever there is a group of Danes at work, at the sports club, even when supposedly letting off steam, group pressure is evident. Danes even applaud in unison.

This code of conformity was first put into words by Aksel Sandemose, a Dane who was so weary of its effects on the people in the area of Jutland where he lived that he broke ranks and moved to Norway. He then wrote a book about life in a fictional Danish town called Jante, which was governed by laws (*loven* = the law) that described the deep-rooted social attitudes he had observed.

The core of Jante's laws is that anyone who sets himself above the rest of the group will be knocked off his perch. There are ten commandments, so similar in nature that one or two are enough to put any would-be Danish individualist squarely in his place:

1. You must not believe that you are anybody.
2. You must not believe you are as important as us.
3. You must not believe you are cleverer than us.
4. You must not deceive yourself that you are better than us.
5. You must not believe that you know more than us.
6. You must not believe that you are more than us.
7. You must not think that you are good at anything.
8. You must not laugh at us.
9. You must not think that anyone cares about you.
10. You must not believe that you can teach us anything.

The code is so ingrained in the Danish mind that a good many believe it originated in the Middle Ages. In fact, it was written in 1933. Though created in irony, these codes have become crystallized in a set of modern-day values every bit as entrenched as the fictitious ones:

1. You must believe everybody is somebody.
2. You must believe everyone is as important as everyone else.
3. You may be cleverer, but that does not make you a better person.
4. You must believe everyone is as good as you.
5. You must believe everyone knows something worth knowing.
6. You must think of everyone as your equal.
7. You must believe everyone can be good at something.
8. You must not laugh at others.
9. You must think everyone is equally worth caring about.
10. You can learn something from everyone.

Every now and again the media focuses on the question of whether *Janteloven* still exists. Although many people say it no longer does, Danish behaviour proves that *Janteloven* is alive and kicking. For example, if an author is naïve enough to give a fellow Dane a manuscript of a story he is writing, the Dane will read it, give it back and say, "I read another book about the same subject last year." He will then proceed to describe it in detail.

If someone works hard and earns enough money to buy a beautiful car, the minute he parks it in the driveway the questions begin. "Is it a company car?", "Bought it second-hand, did you?", "Someone leave you a little legacy then?" – the reason being that no one should be so good at something that they earn more money than anyone else.

People just don't burst in on their friends, brimming with excitement and announce "Guess what, I've just won a contract to sell a new kind of water softener!" They walk in looking tired-out and announce that they've just come back from a really tough meeting. They then wait to have the good news drawn out of them like a rotten tooth.

The spirit of *Janteloven* makes life difficult for Danish copywriters. Companies do not like to draw attention to their achievements or point out their strengths. They feel uncomfortable saying they made a 'healthy' profit, and hate using personal pronouns such as 'we'. They would rather use the name of the company in every sentence of a brochure. This tactic is believed to distance the accomplishments made from the people who made them and results in a tone which is palatably modest.

Another strategy is to write the whole brochure in the passive, e.g:

> *'Production and distribution to 100 countries are co-ordinated from Denmark'* means: 'We produce and distribute goods efficiently and reliably via our network of companies in 100 countries worldwide'.

For similar reasons long sentences with plenty of words are often preferred. The active element is buried, e.g:

> *'A prerequisite for effective planning and management is an understanding of the biological, sedimentary and hydraulic processes, combined with an identification of the sources for the eco-system'* means: 'Biological, sedimentary and hydraulic processes must be understood and sources for the eco-system identified for planning and management to be effective'.

One word which copywriters are allowed to use in abundance is *'mulighed'*, often translated as 'possibility' but closer to 'opportunity'. From this people are encouraged to think that Denmark is a land of opportunity with Danish products opening up opportunities left, right and centre. The only problem is that the Danes cannot bring themselves to say in print exactly what these are for fear of flagrantly violating *Janteloven*.

Some do their best to point out the negative impact of this group pressure. However, en masse the Danes are content to remain firmly huddled together on the ground, happy to brood the fate and await the downfall of those who dare to fly solo. Either that, or they are too scared to make the first move in case someone below chances to whisper the Danish maxim: 'The higher up a monkey climbs, the more you see of its bottom.'

Attitudes and Values

Danish society is consensual rather than adversarial. The political and legal systems aim at finding agreement rather than disagreement. In Denmark 'alternative' views are mainstream. Television interviewers are tame by foreign standards. Danes try to see the other person's point of view, even though the divorce statistics may suggest that consensus is not always easy to achieve. While it is a liberal society, the high degree of social conformity means that all right-thinking people end up with more or less the same opinions. Differences of opinion are more a matter of degree than of principle.

Co-operation

Danes co-operate. LEGO comes from the Danish words *leg godt* which means 'play well', and this is just what the Danes are good at. They get along well with other people. In any brochure translated for the world market, the word 'co-operation' will appear at least three times per page along with a generous sprinkling of 'joint ventures'.

The ability to co-operate is seen as an admirable quality, worth striving for in its own right. In its heyday, even Christiania – an ecological hippy heaven established in an old military barracks in Copenhagen, with rain-water washing machines, solar panels and humus toilets – had joint, common and shared goals, committees, clubs, and a state-approved local area development plan.

The Danes co-operate not only with their colleagues but also with competitors because working together is regarded as enlightened self-interest. It is an attitude which depends on everyone sharing the same values. Meetings are inevitable, but seldom interminable. Video conferencing has a promising future.

On a national level, important constitutional issues are decided by referenda. These are preceded by plenty of long, involved political debates broadcast at peak television viewing times. Video rental shops look forward to them even if no-one else does.

High Standards

Danes expect high standards in the goods and services they buy. They expect the trains to run on time, the streets to be clean and the tradespeople to know their business, which they do. In a restaurant, Danes are not afraid to complain if things are not to their liking, and the complaint is made without bitterness and received without rancour. The fact that they expect things to be done with *omhu* (care), and do not accept bad service or shoddy goods uncomplainingly, helps to maintain their high standards.

This focus on quality is maintained across the board. A front-page newspaper article told of a gentleman who had visited a 'lady of the night' and had subsequently reported her to the police for 'failing to supply the desired outcome'. The police duly investigated the matter but decided to drop the case when they discovered that the gentleman had been exceedingly drunk at the time and the lady in question had put in an hour's overtime in her efforts to satisfy her customer.

Healthy Living

The Danes are very concerned about what they put into themselves. Any additive of any kind is necessarily bad; foods that are 'natural' and high in fibre are necessarily good. Sugar is another target. Where else would a dentist's waiting room have half-litre fizzy-drink bottles hung up by the neck, displaying 32 lumps of sugar as a warning about the contents? Salt, however, seems to have weathered the storm of public antipathy. It has always been a common preservative in any Danish household. Salt the bacon. Salt the herring. Salt the liquorice. Salt the popcorn. Salt the cycle paths...

There is a general attitude that if vitamins are good, more vitamins are better. However, nothing keeps the Danes from enjoying beer, cakes, butter, cheese, hot dogs from the *pølsevogn* (sausage stand), chocolate and cola. Nor from exporting Danish salami which is such a bright pink, it looks radioactive.

Healthy living includes keeping fit and a lot of Danes attend exercise classes. Every town has its well-equipped sports hall and football pitch. Swimming pools have open-plan showers – you take a shower before pulling on your swimsuit and again after your swim, and there are large signs showing parts of the body targeted in red for an extra hard scrub with your soap-saturated disposable sponge.

Environmental Concern

The Danes have long been concerned as to whether any particular policy or form of behaviour is *miljøvenlig* ('environmentally friendly'). To be *miljøvenlig* is highly socially responsible and is viewed as part of healthy living.

As a result, they sort out their rubbish. They sort out their waste water. They sort out anyone caught dumping in the sea off their wonderful blue-flag, sandy beaches. They take the lead in the use of ozone-friendly chemicals, biodegradable plastics, and minimal packaging.

Some power stations are designed and built to run on waste materials. The use of solar energy and windmills is encouraged by state subsidies, and wind farms – forests of wind generators – are humming into action. Pollution is generally frowned upon. Smoking is not. The atmosphere in many living rooms is thick enough to cure herrings.

If you live in a modern housing estate, your hot water for washing and central heating comes underground via well-insulated pipes from one big, shared boiler. This is much more efficient and more convenient than each house having its own. Heat conservation has long been built-in, with houses having double or even triple glazing, cellars, and cavity and roof insulation as standard. When it comes to conserving heat, the Dane considers it a social duty to keep his house warm.

Local rubbish tips are called 'Recycling Stations' and often a container is available where people can put any items destined for the Scout jumble sale. Most bottles carry a deposit which is redeemed when you return them for recycling. This practice was objected to by the European Commission as putting imported drinks at a disadvantage. The Danes argued the environment was more important than European competition law.

For most Danes one of the advantages of belonging to international organisations like the E.U. is to help solve environmental problems, not cause them. Danish Euroscepticism is based on a concern that Denmark will have to lower its standards on the environment, as well as product safety and food hygiene. The fact that the word 'Euro' is like *'uro'* (meaning trouble, unrest, disquiet and concern) doesn't help either.

Consumers are selective and well informed. They react as one to political issues and take pride in boycotting oil companies, vineyards and beef. Fur is another matter entirely. Even in relatively mild winters, women of all ages emerge on the streets wearing sealskin coats. If questioned, they earnestly explain that they are helping to uphold a traditional native craft which forms the base of the Greenland economy.

Religion

Religious devotion is a regional phenomenon in Denmark. An austere fundamentalism flourishes on the west coast of Jutland in the areas where fishing is the traditional occupation. Until recently, life was hard and short and this was, and still is, reflected in the religious beliefs of these communities.

The official religion of the Danes is Lutheran. Everybody pays church tax unless they specifically opt out, which few do. Since they retain their church membership by paying church taxes, most Danes use it at least four times during their lives, for their baptism, confirmation, marriage (at least once) and funeral.

Confirmations are the most popular religious ritual. Many are more like weddings than weddings themselves with present lists, table plans, elaborate white dresses for the girls and smart outfits for the boys There is even a kind of honeymoon called a 'Blue Monday', which is a day off school for the individual concerned.

Even if religion is not involved, similarly lavish 'nonfirmation' parties are held. Either way, the adolescent becomes the embarrassed centre of attention, both as the squirming object of speeches by maudlin uncles and tearfully cheerful aunts, and the mortified subject of intimate verses composed and sung by his or her family and friends.

The lives of Danes are also influenced by a rather more sombre song-writer, N.F.S. Grundtvig, a priest (and son of a priest), who died in 1872 at the age of nearly 90. In the course of his long life he wrote over

1,400 hymns. He liked to dredge up old Nordic words and bolt them together almost regardless of meaning. For those who like such orotundities, they are just the job, but they may go some way to explaining the generally low church attendance.

Grundtvig described Denmark as the country where 'few have too much and fewer too little'. Apart from his hymns, his lasting legacy was the establishment of Folk High Schools which gave the opportunity of education to tens of thousands of working people including agricultural workers, and are still in existence.

Grundtvig was charismatic, little concerned with orthodox theology and a thorn in the side of the church authorities. However, the unorthodox views of yesterday can today become orthodox; he lived so long and said so many different and contradictory things that it is possible for people of widely differing views to call themselves 'Grundtvigian'. Grundtvigianism, rather like Hinduism, embraces a variety of beliefs.

Happy Families

The Danes love getting married, but Danish marriages lack the famous 'clutching power' of the LEGO brick: Denmark has one of the highest divorce rates in Europe. Marriage can be a necessary preliminary to divorce. Couples will often cohabit for a long time in what are called 'paperless' marriages and will then formalise the arrangement before getting divorced. It is as if formalising a stable arrangement destabilises it.

Denmark was the first country in Europe to allow a form of marriage for homosexuals. This is a reflection of the generally liberal attitude which allows people to lead their lives as they choose, as long as it does not bother others. No-one twitches an eyebrow at those who choose to share their morning newspaper prior to marriage, and a couple's children will often attend their wedding.

A high proportion of babies are born to unmarried parents. This is not to say that babies born to unmarried parents are born outside a stable relationship, nor that, given the high divorce rate, babies born to married parents are born within a stable relationship. In fact, it makes little or no difference to the children whether the parents are married or not. Whatever their relationship or its stability, most Danish children spend most of their waking hours being brought up by someone else.

Share Care

A dominant factor of family life is that most parents go out to work. High house prices and high taxation mean they can't afford not to. There is widespread provision of maternity and paternity leave, crèches, nursery schools, childcare centres, and so on. All this leaves women equally free to continue their studies or pursue a meaningful, socially relevant career after they have become parents, and because of the back-up systems there is little excuse not to.

In many areas, housing estates are like ghost towns during the working day – except for some harassed adults shepherding long crocodiles of small children coming and going from local places of interest. King-size prams with two small occupants and one or two hangers-on also feature in the street scene. The poor women pushing what can amount to 80lbs of weight are not the victims of over-effective fertility treatment programmes. They are council-approved 'daycare mummies'.

'Baby bio' at some cinemas is more for mothers than their babies. Liberated mums time their babies' naps just right, park their prams in the foyer, collect a numbered ticket and go in to watch the film. They might not hear much of it though because every so often a head pops round the door and calls "Number 6 your child is up", and all around you in the semi-darkness are the sounds of the gentle hicks and guzzlings of babies breast-feeding.

Children are placed in daycare institutions from the age of about six months. Later on, other daycare institutions take over at the end of the school day, and children are entertained until their parents appear to collect them. As a result, during the week they get a homogenised upbringing provided by trained pedagogues, while their parents try to balance the conflicting demands of work and family. At the weekend parents attempt to squeeze a week's worth of love and affection into two days.

Parental discipline is liberal. Good social behaviour is exhorted. Anti-social behaviour is discouraged by whichever responsible adult is closest and is sometimes rebuked but never chastised, as striking a child is illegal. Conflicts are normally nipped firmly in the bud before they escalate past the "My Dads are bigger than your Dads*" stage.

The Elderly

Elderly Danes are independent and have lives of their own. They are issued with a *Mimrekort* ('dodderers' card') which gives cheap access to public transport, theatres, cinemas, museums, and evening classes in the daytime. Add to this daycare centres and home helps, and as long as the old stay healthy and alert, life can be fun.

Working mothers with offspring too sick to attend school are lucky if granny is available for babysitting.

*With the number of changes of partners there is a plurality of Mums and Dads – all except the natural ones being referred to as '*pap*' (cardboard) figures.

This explains the *'mormor ordning'* (grandma scheme) advertised in some kindergartens. Parents pay to sign their children up for the scheme and then kindly old ladies help out as granny stand-ins.

When they get too old or frail to look after themselves, grannies and grandads are shuffled off to suitably *hyggelige* old folks homes. Ordinary family housing is not designed for extended families. Also, with changing patterns of marriage, what obligation does someone have to look after his or her stepmother's second husband, or his third wife? People have enough to do sorting out pillow cases for their stepchildren without coping with their stepchildren's stepgrandparents.

Family Names

The Danes take naming their children very seriously. Though they have a few names in mind before the birth, parents often wait until the baby's personality begins to show before registering their final choice.

Most Danish surnames end in -sen, for example, Hansen ('Hans's son'). Surnames only became general about the middle of the 19th century. Until then if Hans had a son and called him Jens, he would be known as Jens Hansen. If Jens Hansen then had a son, and called him Hans, he would be called Hans Jensen. At some point it became customary for people to stick with the family name they had, and pass it on to their children. This is why many Danish surnames are so similar, Jensen, Hansen, Larsen, Nielsen.

Many women keep their maiden names in marriage, which enables them to retain their identity in cases of serial monogamy. Children inherit these double-barrelled names. If they meet a double-barrelled partner, they then have the choice of four surnames. This is easier than it sounds when two are likely to be Jensen or Hansen.

The Fabric of Society

Dress codes exist but they are situation-specific. Children do not wear school uniform, but they don't need to: from the age of six months they are dressed alike anyway. For comfort, and the convenience of the child-minder, clothing is index-linked to the weather forecast. By the time children start school, parents are fully aware of the advantages of investing in practical, washable, 100% waterproof, thermal, wool-lined garments that fasten with Velcro tapes. This rather narrows down the field of choice. Needless to say, nametapes are also obligatory – forenames included. Hold up a stray item and call out "A. Jensen" and a forest of little hands shoots up.

In later life, dress codes can become more subtle. Once again, integration is the key. A female computer engineer must be careful not to look too smart or she could be mistaken for a secretary. A building consultant must look casual enough to be regarded by the labourers as one of the team, but smart enough to represent management.

Though a class system as such does not exist, colour coding is widespread in Denmark. Gardeners wear green or brown overalls, carpenters wear beige. Manual workers wear blue and though strictly speaking bleach and solvents are not environmentally friendly, bricklayers and painters wear white.

Material possessions are also a pretty good indicator of status. That, and the height of your flag pole.

Wealth and Status

Being average in Denmark is respectable, even desirable. Success is a solitary pleasure not to be publicly flaunted. Snobbery about jobs is almost non-existent and most people can afford the everyday luxuries of life. Being ambitious and making money is fine, but sending your children to fee-paying schools (of which there are a handful in Denmark) is not. It is considered bad form to buy privilege over and above what the State provides and to stand out from the crowd in any way is considered a dangerous threat to the holy creeds of *hygge* and *Jante*.

Wealthier Danes have a hard time getting rid of their money in a socially acceptable way. They can spend it on clothes and perfume, a good hairdo and designer goods of all descriptions. Jewellery, amber (the precious stone of Denmark), furniture and household items are all acceptable, provided they are stylish in a Scandinavian way. But a fine line has to be trodden to avoid the Curse of *Jante*, not to mention the attentions of the taxman.

Snobbery does rear its head in Danish society, though chiefly among the young. Woe betide the 14-year-old without the right designer clothes and trainers. This imported trend is a plague to parents, who complain to each other about the Danish youth of today over a cup of coffee poured from their new, Italian-designed, £190 coffee pot.

Manners and Behaviour

The Danes have confidently liberated themselves from the petty forms of etiquette and the residue of subservience to superiors which still passes for manners in other societies. They are not hamstrung by politeness and are more likely to step in to deal with a potentially embarrassing situation than the English. When confronted with obnoxious lunatics, epilepsy attacks and the victims of street violence, the average Englishman will purse his lips like a prune and scurry across to the other side of the road. A Dane will steam in shamelessly and clear up the mess.

They don't say they are sorry. If a customer rings and asks to speak to Mr. Jensen, a Dane may simply reply "Mr. Jensen is not in". "I'm sorry" doesn't come into it. He is not sorry. He is quite glad Mr. Jensen is out putting his skills to good use.

They cannot be blamed however for the fact that the word 'please' simply does not exist in Danish. Children are taught to say 'Bede om' (literally 'ask for') instead. For example, "May I ask for another lollipop?" Either way, the answer is the same.

They say what they think about sex, politics, religion, everything. Small talk can assume monstrous proportions. They will tell you frankly how much their mortgage is, how much they earn per hour and whether or not they shave their armpits. They will ask you equally frankly "Is it hot in here or is it just my menopause?", or, "How old are you, Hillary? You don't mind me calling you Hillary, do you, Mrs. Clinton?"

They do not appreciate lateness. When they are invited to a social gathering at a specified time, they turn up strictly when invited, if not before. So someone who has invited a Dane as a guest should not be relaxing in the bath at the appointed hour. It is considered impolite to keep others waiting. Anyone excusing themselves for being more than a few minutes late for a business meeting will be greeted with a droll "It happens", the inference being that it may happen, but not to me.

Punctuality may also help explain what appears to be thoughtlessness. Doors are seldom held open for the person following behind and motorists hardly ever let other drivers join the stream of traffic. The feeling is that "If they want to be where I am now, they should have got out of bed five seconds earlier."

Queuing is disliked. Nothing makes a Dane happier than if an additional checkout opens and he can beat other contenders to the conveyor belt. No-one bats an eyelid. In Britain the person concerned would be strung up by his sausages, but not in Denmark.

The custom of removing footwear before entering the house has more to do with leaving heelmarks in wooden floorboards than anything else. At parties high heels are greeted with shocked silence. Fortunately few people wear them. Firstly they are ergonomically questionable and, secondly, so many streets are composed of cobblestones or granite sets that you would be more likely to end up at Casualty than the party in question.

When making telephone calls, Danes politely begin by stating their name which means that instead of saying "This is Mr. Skjoldbøl", a Dane says his or her full name and uses the Danish 'it' form, e.g., "It is Bent Skjoldbøl." This leaves a foreigner on the other end wondering if it is indeed a name, and, if so, how he can politely ask the Dane to repeat it slowly enough for him to grasp it.

Dressing for the occasion is also important. Turning up for a confirmation straight from the pub with yesterday's jeans, malodorous T-shirt and greying trainers is very bad form. It's not turning up straight from the pub that raises eyebrows, it's not having bothered to shower and change beforehand.

Toasting Others

In Denmark spirits are raised collectively. At a meal with other people, rather than picking up your glass and drinking from it, it is customary to drink a *skål* (pronounced 'skole', and roughly translated as 'cheers'). What this entails is picking up the glass, catching the eye of someone else, raising the glass to head height, waiting for anyone else who wants to join in, looking round at all who are involved, raising the glass a couple of inches higher, and saying "*Skål*", before bringing the glass to your mouth. In reverse order, the glass is taken from the mouth and held up head-high, everyone involved looks round at everyone else, smiles and nods approvingly, and the glass is replaced on the table, ready for the process to begin again.

It would be bad manners not to drink when so encouraged, and for a guest it is good manners to single out one's host and hostess and drink a *skål* with them, and with the people on either side, and the people opposite, and with anyone else who may have been previously omitted. A person can get pie-eyed in no time.

Greetings

Danes are not great social kissers. For most purposes a handshake will do. The frequency of handshaking in Denmark lies somewhere between the English, who do it once in a lifetime, and the French who shake hands whenever they have been out of the room. When something more than a handshake is required, Danes adopt a non-kissing embrace. There is no facial contact, just a dignified leaning together of the upper halves of the body, and maybe a mutual clapping on the back.

Third-party introductions are unheard of. When attending a private gathering, after handing over flowers, chocolates or bottle of wine to their hosts, Danes will go round and introduce themselves to everyone present. It is well recognised that at this stage no conversation is struck up which will prevent the new arrivals from completing their tour of introduction.

This custom can cause problems for Danes attending functions abroad. If the host is busy, the Danish guest may simply walk through the door, stride up to a complete stranger, grasp his hand and shake it vigorously while announcing his name. Foreigners find this a bit unexpected. Englishmen have been known to stare straight through the Dane as if he isn't there.

At the end of an evening, Danes will go round the

guests again and take their leave. This fosters a sense of everyone being at the same party.

When meeting, people cover themselves for any recent hospitality by saying *"Tak for sidst"* (Thank you for the last time). And when meeting part of a family group it is usual to ask them to *Hils* (say hello to) the other members of the family. Originally it was customary to say, for example, *"Hils* Jens" or *"Hils* Karen" but naming the name is now optional. This is convenient when "Say hello to your wife" is risky enough.

Forms of Address

Despite the general lack of formality in Danish life, there is one area in which Danes retain an almost ceremonial correctness, and that is in including a person's professional occupation when addressing them.

So when filling in forms – for example, to open a bank account – the applicant will state his or her occupation. Bank statements and circulars will then be addressed either to: 'Fr. (Ms.) Karen Hansen' or *Biblioteks-assistent* Karen Hansen (Library Assistant Karen Hansen). As she progresses through her career Ms. Hansen must make sure to inform the bank when she becomes successively *Bibliotekar* (Librarian), *Overbibliotekar* (Senior Librarian), *Stadsbibliotekar* (Chief Librarian) and finally in retirement *Fhv. Stadsbibliotekar* (Former Chief Librarian Karen Hansen).

There are three possible reasons why this formality persists in an otherwise informal society. The first is that people train for so long to obtain their professional qualification that they identify strongly with their occupation and are proud of it. The second is that there are so many people called Karen Hansen that something is needed to distinguish between Karen Hansen the library assistant, and Karen Hansen the sales consultant. The third is that

Danes do this as a matter of habit, and have never thought not to.

The use of the formal 'you' – *De* for both singular and plural – has almost disappeared, though it still persists among the very old and in the most expensive shops and restaurants. It is also useful for taking the high ground when making customer complaints.

Leisure and Pleasure

Time Off

In spring, the most beautiful place to be is in a beech forest, striding through the carpet of white anemones with the sun shining through the fresh lime-green canopy. In summer, woodland clearings are perfect for sand-free picnics, and in autumn all you need is a basket to go scuffing about in the glorious gold, red, and russet leaves hunting for mushrooms.

Foreign package-tour holidays are as popular with Danes as they are with other nations. But holidays at home are still top of the list, with a peculiarly Danish institution known as the summer house. These are to be found wherever there is a beach, sprouting like fungus around seaside villages. Sometimes there is a whole complex of them, with warrens of streets and skeletons of postmen who died trying to find their way out of the maze.

A typical summer house is made of wood to give the impression of ruggedness. It is a small affair, roughly the size of a two-roomed flat, with a garden to match. The majority were knocked up in the boom period of the early 1970s and were definitely not built to last. As they are only used for a few weeks each year this doesn't seem to matter that much to the owners, who potter around in a caricature of practical efficiency doing things with creosote and garden tools that they never have time to do at home.

Danes who live in the city and have no garden or summer house may escape to soak up the sun with friends in a *kolonihave* – a cheerful allotment garden with a beautifully tended hut (a sort of Wendy-house for adults) – where the flag is flown when the owners are in residence.

Boating

The Danes have always been a seafaring people. Their clapboard buildings and love of bare floorboards in their houses and apartments could be said to reflect a hankering for the planking of the old Viking longships.

On any fine summer weekend day, with the sun shining and breezes blowing, the marinas will be packed with boats. There are hundreds of islands and harbours, and nowhere in Denmark is far from the sea.

Boats are immensely popular, but there is a distinction between 'boats' and 'boating', ownership being considerably more widespread than the activity. All through the summer, Danes with a real or imagined nautical bent will be found scrubbing and polishing their precious hulls, gazing jealously at the bigger vessels in the marina while sneering at the lesser ones. They may swap the suburban garden fence for the rails of a boat, but their values are the same.

For those who bravely put out to sea in their gleaming craft, sailing combines everything that Danes hold dear: fresh air, a pollution-free energy source, stylish but practical waterproof Helly Hansen clothing and the feeling of being part of a crew working in unison towards a common goal. Plus, the mast is comfortingly like a flag pole.

Dog-walking

Dog-owning in Denmark is taken seriously, and many owners attend training sessions. Everyone is good at time management, so dogs live life in the fast lane too, running alongside bicycles to get their exercise instead of being taken for walks. '*I snor*' ('on a lead') notices are common, but there are few other dog traces to be seen. The Danes were pioneers of the custom of dog owners taking plastic bags on dog walks, for doing what dog owners do with plastic bags on dog walks.

Football

Danish football has two problems. One is that though there are some very fine Danish football players, most of the best ones play for foreign clubs because they pay better than Danish ones. The other is that many leading Danish football clubs have names such as AB, FCK, AaB and OB, which sound more like Treasury bonds than anything to cheer for.

The greatest asset of Danish football, apart from some very good players, is the fans. They behave with good humour and sporting enthusiasm and are known as *roligans* (from *rolig* meaning still or quiet). This may be because it is impossible to work up a blood-lust for a team called B93.

Denmark has never really returned to earth after winning the European Cup in 1992. Qualifying for the final brought the whole country to such a fever pitch that some Danish passengers actually managed to persuade the captain of a flight from Norway to Copenhagen to fly over the stadium while the game was in progress.

Quite a few schools allow important qualifying games to be shown, but some employers are less sympathetic. One manager who watched a 2002 World Cup match during his lunch hour was subsequently given the boot.

Cycling

Danes identify with their cycling sporting heroes because most of them use bicycles every day. Bicycles are not only the most *miljøvenlige* form of transport, but good for the *kondi* (from *kondition*, meaning 'fitness').

Through the years the nation has produced a succession of Olympic medallists and stage winners in international competitions. When Bjarne Riis became the first Dane to win the Tour de France, people everywhere ran out and painted his name in white paint on the road. They then raced off to buy themselves the essential gear, from water containers to shiny saddle-padded cycling shorts, before hopping on to their bikes to join the ranks of cycling fanatics. They can still be seen hurtling along Danish roads with their jersey pockets back to front for aerodynamic purposes.

Winter Sports

There is only one genuine winter sport in Denmark. It is played early in the morning, against the clock, with small hand-held implements called car windscreen scrapers.

The rest are summer sports played indoors. Handball, badminton, indoor tennis, indoor hockey – any excuse to join a club and have a bit of fun during the long winter evenings. Consequently Denmark has produced a long string of male and female world and All-England Champions.

Winter lasts as long as the other three seasons put together. Not only is it long, it can be gloomy. In midwinter it never gets entirely light (while in midsummer it never gets entirely dark). Though the temperature hovers about freezing point, Denmark does not have the requisite snow, ice or mountains for outdoor winter sports. There is always enough snow to inconvenience traffic and to bring shovelling householders out on to the pavements, but seldom enough for fun. When there is, everyone who can do so grabs a motley collection of skis and toboggans and heads for anything resembling a hill.

Though the highest point in Denmark is actually Yding Skovhøj at 173 metres, it is popularly believed that this honour belongs to Himmelbjerget, the ironically named 'Heaven Mountain'. Danes seem to have a low expectation of heaven because it is only 147 metres high, not much higher than St. Peter's in Rome.

Tivoli

Tivoli is a pleasure garden in the middle of Copenhagen. But it is not simply that: it is a magical part of the Danes' childhood experience.

By day it offers a garden with flowers and fountains, a lake with a full-sized galleon, cafés and restaurants, swings, rides, roundabouts, and clowns – a place for old-age pensioners to sit having coffee and cakes and watch small children eating candyfloss, wide-eyed with wonder. By night, it becomes a fairyland of glow lamps with a concert hall, the Tivoli Garden Guard (a children's marching band), a theatre for revues, acrobatic shows, an open-air pantomime with Harlequin and Columbine, ghost trains, big dippers, beer halls with communal singing, popcorn, ice cream, and fireworks.

Tivoli has been thriving for over 150 years, maintaining a balance between well-loved traditions and the latest in entertainment; between robust fun and simple enjoyment. It is the embodiment of innocent pleasure, where everyone can slip away for a while from the serious business of being adult.

Drinking and Eating

Danes are Olympic drinkers – it even says so in *Hamlet*. It is possible to buy drink without difficulty 24 hours a day, seven days a week, throughout Denmark – even at petrol stations.

There are any number of cafés in all Danish towns, where people go to drink hot chocolate, play backgammon and have a free read of the papers. Those who love the tabloids, but are too abashed to buy them, get their fix in a café. Apart from backgammon, the Danes play games with dice, generally for drinks.

Alcohol is expensive. The favoured spirit is either *snaps*, which is potato-based, or a concoction called *Gammel Dansk* (Old Danish). Some Danes like a shot of this soon after rising as a quick snifter to set them up for the day. It provides fortification against a cold winter's morning (even in summer). The fact that it tastes like cough medicine backs up the claim that it does you good.

Beer

What oil is to Texas, beer is to Denmark. Something like 284 million litres of Danish beer are exported annually – over half a billion pints.

The first thing you notice about a Dane is that he always has a bottle opener handy. Drinks are sold mainly in bottles rather than cans for recycling purposes. Trolleys full of empties are trundled quite openly through shopping centres. No-one feels obliged to explain that they have just had a party or cleared out their garage.

Full or empty, transporting crates is heavy work, especially on a bike, so many will save themselves the trouble by disposing of the beer immediately outside the supermarkets.

Apart from Carlsberg and Tuborg, there are many local brewers and each brewery has its supporters, almost as if it were a football team. The beers come in different strengths; some are very strong, especially the Export beers which happily do not all get exported. Weaker (light) beers which have a low alcohol content are popularly known as 'cissies' beer'.

Carlsberg and Tuborg, though regarded as rivals, are owned by the same company and even come from the same brewery. In the old days the more academically or philanthropically minded would drink their beer either in the cause of art or in the cause of science, because Carlsberg was a great contributor to the arts and Tuborg to scientific research. Now it's purely a matter of taste.

Breweries bring out special beers every year at Easter and Christmas. University lecturers know all about 'P-day', the day when the Påske (Easter) beer hits the streets and the students; and the launch of Tuborg's *'snebajer'* (snow beer) in mid-November is a cause for national celebration. Danes everywhere wait impatiently for one minute to twelve on the appointed day. *Snebajer* beer coincides with the season of office Christmas parties held by the vast majority of companies on a Friday afternoon and followed by a weekend of alcohol-induced cold turkey.

All manner of bad behaviour is tolerated if the transgressor is in his cups. In fact, not letting one's hair down at a party is to risk being called a spoilsport. However, Danes expect people to hold their drink, which is why they are so contemptuous of the Swedes whose alcoholic excesses they consider to be beyond the pale. In a Carlsberg advertisement, a typical Swede had to agree not to urinate in a public place, make obscene gestures to Danish girls, be sick on the pavement or fall asleep on the bus to the ferry, before he was allowed to drink Danish beer.

The un-Danish Pastry

In Denmark the 'Danish pastry' is known neither as Danish nor as pastry. It is called *wienerbrød*, which means Viennese bread, though it is neither Viennese nor bread.

Every baker's window is stuffed with these glazed confections, as well as cakes, tarts, rolls and biscuits. Each tempting creation has its own specific name, for example: snail, goose breast, frog snapper, gallop kringle, and one, which oozes custard, called a baker's bad eye. This may help to explain why a clever marketing executive somewhere cooked up the all-embracing term 'Danish pastry'.

Bacon

'Danish' bacon is produced almost entirely for the export market and goes by the name of 'English' bacon (with lots of meat) and 'Irish' bacon (more fat, less meat). The Danes eat a lot of pork, some of it cured, but he who seeks bacon in Denmark may find himself offered a squarish slab of something dark and forbidding which calls itself bacon, but is bacon in name only. Nor are pigs to be seen anywhere in the countryside. Denmark has almost twice as many pigs as people, but the pigs are invisible.

Typical Meals

The best thing about breakfast is the freshly baked rolls. Even in the dead of winter on Sunday mornings the menfolk shrug on their overcoats and brave the elements on their way to the baker's and battle home with paper bags bursting with bread and sweet pastries for their families.

Standard fare at lunch is the open sandwich, *smørrebrød*, literally meaning 'bread and butter'. There is, however, precious little bread involved. What there is looks like a small square of doormat with the bristles shaved off. Made of rye (which stays fresh for much longer than white bread), it's the base for a vast variety of toppings: mild cheese with peppers, celery and grapes or walnuts; strong cheese with radishes; salted beef with horseradish and pickles; smoked eel with scrambled egg and watercress; pickled herring with hard boiled egg; pickled herring with capers and raw onion rings; the outrageous '*stjerneskud*' (shooting star) – a mound of shrimps, mayonnaise, fried fish and slices of tropical fruit, garnished with dill and a twist of lemon... Hybrids include the '*klap sammen*' ('smacked together') which is like the English sandwich, but with a filling one can actually taste.

The *smørrebrød* favoured above all others is *dyrlægens natmad* (a *dyrlæge* is a veterinary surgeon). It consists of liver pâté on sourdough bread with a layer of meat jelly crowned with a slice of salted meat. No-one knows why such a dish is called a Vet's Supper; it could equally well be called a dog's breakfast.

The main meal of the day is eaten between 6 and 7 o'clock. It starts early and is dealt with efficiently, sandwiched between work, school, society meetings and other activities. Danes are fond of meat: sausage or meatballs are cheap favourites, or roast pork. A traditional dish called *brændende kærlighed* (burning love) consists of crispy bacon pieces served in their own fat and poured over mashed potatoes. Vegetarians have a hard time. Even the larger supermarkets do not respond to their demands. They are more likely to come away from the frozen food cabinets with frostbite than a ready made meal.

On special occasions, meals are allocated much longer. In fact guests at large-scale parties generally linger until the official signal to depart arrives in the guise of *natmad* (literally 'night food'). By the time this snack is served, even the most enthusiastic hostess is glancing at the clock and itching to get the coffee stains off her pine table. Roughly translated, *natmad* means 'eat up and push off'.

The Rite of the Cold Table

The true heart of Danish culinary arts is not in any particular dish, but in the whole concept and execution of the cold table. The basic elements are: the bread, the *pålæg* (meaning the things that are put on the bread), and the *tilbehør* (i.e., the accessories, or the things that are put on the things that are put on the bread). But you wouldn't dream of putting just anything with anything. The right *tilbehør* should be used with the right *pålæg*, and the right *pålæg* should be used with the right bread.

The dishes must be taken in the right order: first the marinated herring, then the red herring and the herring in curry sauce, all of this on rye bread. (Herring (*sild*) is so popular that the same word is used for a tasty young lady.) Next come shrimps with mayonnaise on white bread. Then a little *gravad laks* with mustard sauce on white bread with caraway seeds.

Meanwhile, beer has been served, and a *skål* has been drunk. Then a *snaps* is poured, a welcoming speech is made by the host, and a *snapse skål* is drunk. The used plates are taken out and clean plates brought in along with a warm dish, meat balls with cucumber salad, or a breaded fillet of plaice with Danish *remoulade* (a relish used with everything from fish to junk food).

All the time the food is eaten with the right accompaniments on the right plate with the right cutlery, an eye has to be kept open for the entrance of fresh dishes or the need to join in the drinking of a *skål*.

In between mouthfuls, guests are expected to remember to make appreciative comments about the food. Then it's on through the prepared salads to the cheese, and a free market for making speeches and *skål*. Finally everyone retires from the table to drink coffee and cognac and fill in any remaining gaps with small cakes.

A well-executed cold table is a genuine piece of Danish heritage, where the guests are active performers in a shared ritual.

Custom and Tradition

Christmas

Christmas is the major festival of the year, and Danish children believe that Father Christmas comes from Greenland. Whole families go out into the woods to fell their own carefully chosen fir tree, and collect moss and natural treasures. They then use every scrap of glue, fabric, wool and imagination to turn beech nuts, egg boxes and anything else into troll-like creatures called *nisser*.

Each house has its own real *nisse* who lives all the year round out of sight in the attic. However these mischievous beings only become active in December. They play tricks, leave small advent presents in stockings, and generally remind the family below that *nisser* cause trouble if they don't get their portion of festive rice pudding (with a dollop of butter) the night before Christmas. For the entire month, a *nisse* programme glues children to the television and each day they are given *kalendar* gifts – sweets, pens, hair bobbles, keyrings – anything from the toyshop bargain buckets that will last out the day.

On Christmas Eve, before joining hands and circling the tree (hung with plaited paper hearts, and often lit with real candles), the family sit down to roast duck, roast potatoes and red cabbage, and plenty of it. Several help-ings are passed around before the rice pudding is served – with lashings of cream and hot cherry sauce. A surprise almond is hidden in the pudding and the person who finds it can lay claim to a present, usually a marzipan pig. Unenlightened foreign visitors have been known to eat the almond, unaware of its significance, thus forcing the rest of the company to work its way through the whole pudding in search of the elusive nut.

One custom that the Danes have made into something special is *Julefrokost*, the office Christmas lunch. Unlike the family party, this innocent-sounding event starts out as an informal occasion. Games are played, songs are only sung if people want to (strangely enough they often do) and office flirtations are carried on in a rather more open manner than before. After a respectable time lapse, all manner of gross indecency is tolerated. The sight of 600 shipyard workers naked, weeping, fighting and dancing on the tables at 3 o'clock in the afternoon was too much for one young welder. He has not been to a *Julefrokost* since.

Other Celebrations

Danes ring in the New Year with a bang. Millennium celebrations saw many exceeding the 5 kilo limit per household on 'explosives'. Fortunately, few accidents occur – the only dangerously short fuses belong to neighbours who forget to sedate their cats, dogs or horses.

Fastelavn is held in early February. Once upon a time a barrel was hung from a rope, and inside the barrel was a cat; the young blades of the area would take it in turns to gallop past the barrel on horseback and give it a hearty passing thwack with a stout club. The man who hit it hard enough to make the cat fall out won the game.

These days the cat is a cut-out pasted on the barrel, and the local children take turns to hit it with a club; when the bottom falls out so do the sweets, enough not just for the 'winner' but for everyone. More importantly this is the chance for children to dress up. Television characters, monsters, fairy-tale heroes, the question is not "What do you want to be when you grow up?" it is "What do you want to be for *Fastelavn*?" For children this is the day that dreams come true. For parents it can be a last-minute nightmare: Disney costumes sell out fast.

Danes still commemorate the ending of the Second World War in Denmark on 4th May 1945. That evening, with the ending of the blackout, someone lit a candle in a window and the idea spread like wildfire throughout the land. Each year since, on the same day, many repeat this simple silent tribute.

St. Hans Eve, on the longest day of the year, is the time when people build bonfires, preferably on the seashore. As the sun sinks, traditional songs are sung and fires are lit in an attempt to keep the sun's flames alive, and stop the year turning to winter. The highlight of the evening is when the homemade witch on top of the bonfire catches light and 'flies' off to the home of all witches, Brocken Mountain in Germany. It can be a stirring sight to see a chain of bonfires stretching along the coast on a still summer's evening, and to feel a sense of community with people all over the country who are doing the same thing. *Hygge* on a national scale.

Anniversaries

Silver weddings are celebrated in style. In country districts all the neighbours fly the *Dannebrog*, and friends gather in the early morning at the home of the happy couple. A triumphal arch of branches is placed about their door, a group of top-hatted horn players appears, and the celebrants are surprised in their beds by a serenade played and sung outside their window. However, the happy couple should not be so surprised that they haven't organised a hearty breakfast for anyone who may turn up.

Half way to the silver wedding is the copper wedding, commemorated after twelve and a half years of marriage, and so not on the relevant date at all. It is not certain whether Danes do this due to their love of celebration, or due to pessimism about the prospects of couples hanging on for 25 years.

Employers celebrate when their employees have worked for them for a significant number of years. Local newspapers acknowledge those celebrating round birthdays (ones with a 0 or even a 5), anniversaries and retirements with a page full of toothy grins and embarrassing snap shots sent in by relatives and so-called friends. Ageing gracefully is not easy in the glare of such publicity.

Sense of Humour

Danish humour suffers from the handicap of the Danes' literal-mindedness ("Can you play the violin?" "I don't know, I've never tried."), and from their need to conform. In a country where all right-thinking people think the right things, no-one is sufficiently different to laugh at.

Popular Danish humour tends to be victimless. Biting political satire is not widespread as there is so little to bite on in Danish politics. Teasing is acceptable, as long as the object of the teasing goes along with it, but really savage attacks, even on the rich and famous, are virtually non-existent. To take things so far is considered un-*hyggelig* and therefore frowned upon.

Sarcasm and self-deprecation are likely to be misunderstood. No-one dares say they are better than anyone else, but no-one would say they were worse. The person who says "My cakes always rise like an arthritic elephant" will be told quite earnestly "That's not true. You made a very nice sponge cake for us the Easter before last."

Danes have a weakness for slapstick. For them Dirch Passer was the archetypal buffoon. In his film comedy about national service, he rushes out of the barracks late for parade and his trousers fall down. Danes are carried out of the cinema weeping with laughter.

The last word in classic Danish comedy is a particular revue sketch from the 1960s, *Babs and Nutte*. The scene is a doctor's consulting room. A buxom woman enters and starts describing her problems with Babs and Nutte to the doctor (played by Dirch Passer). For 20 minutes a huge double entendre is played out in which the patient keeps referring to Babs and Nutte which the doctor thinks are her breasts. They are, of course, not her breasts, but her two pet dogs. Foreigners presented with this irresistible thigh-slapper are fixed with a war-like look and put to the question along the lines of "Come on, you must admit this is hilarious!"

Humour of a more sophisticated and zany kind, such as *Monty Python*, is also popular, being highly visual, witty and clownish, but where the 'victims' of the humour do not need the sympathy of the viewer, which enables the Danes to enjoy guilt-free laughter.

The best Danish humour is whimsical, almost surrealistic. A well-known exponent of this was Storm P., a comic whose cartoons are still in print. There is even a museum of his work. Here are some examples:

"Have you been punished before?"
"No, only afterwards."

"One often thinks about something, which, on reflection, turns out to be… unthinkable."

"What did the Doctor say?"
"He said I needed to take things easy. That makes me uneasy."

And for the truly surrealistic:

"Do you like oysters?"

"Yes, with red cabbage."
"I said, do you like oysters?"
"Yes, with red cabbage."

Storm P. was famous for cartoons featuring tramps who delighted in names like Sophocles and Pericles. One of these went: Sophocles: "Tell me, Pericles, when does a Tuborg taste best?" Pericles: "Always!" This caption became one of the most enduring advertisements for the product.

Stand-up comedy is becoming more and more popular in Denmark, though it takes courage for a Dane to stand up alone in the spotlight when everyone else is sitting down. It is here that more vicious satire is presented. Comedies with stereotyped characters recognised from the different regions of the country go down a treat. The Jutland peasant and the loud-mouth Copenhagener, with the obligatory Danish sex-bomb thrown in for good measure, are a guaranteed hit.

There is also one group of people about whom it is acceptable to make jokes. The people of Copenhagen make the same kind of jokes about the people of Århus, based on their pretended lack of intelligence, that the English make about the Irish or the Americans about the Poles. For example: "Why do police cars in Århus need two police-men?" Answer: "Because they have a two-tone horn."

Humour in everyday life is low-key, which may have something to do with Denmark being a largely rural country. The misfortunes of those who bring down the Curse of *Jante*, the antics of the neighbourhood *særling* (eccentric), plus local gossip are always good for a few laughs. For example, a miser invested his fortune in the building of a large crayfish farm 15 miles from a colony of herons, a protected species in Denmark. Villagers would drive miles out of their way to catch a glimpse of the farmer brandishing his shotgun in impotent fury while herons waded serenely in his private lakes, picking off his life's savings one by one.

Culture

Design

Danish design is famed for its lightness and elegance. Large wooden coffee tables seem to float on thin air and flights of stairs appear to take flight. Designer *brugskunst* (the art of the usable) fetches high prices in furniture, lighting, textiles, silverware, porcelain, and so forth. Some objects are such classics of design and form that newly-qualified Danish furniture designers complain of manufacturers not being interested in trying new ideas. The furniture of Arne Jacobsen and the lamps of Poul Henningsen (who were both distinguished architects) are still produced and exported in large quantities even though these designs date from the early 1950s. Erik Jørgensen's sofas and Hans Wegner's wooden chairs have been sought after for decades, as have Nanna Ditzel's ring chairs – though it seems Danish designers would sometimes rather spend time designing their furniture than sitting back on it and relaxing. Which could explain why comfort occasionally takes a back seat.

In the hands of a Dane even the definition of the humble kitchen tap is open to interpretation. These sculptures of 'Anguish in Stainless Steel' are often a combination of chunky tubes, spouts and angled levers which have to be pushed, pulled, twisted or swivelled with care to avoid an unexpected jet of boiling or freezing water.

Timeless designs include the label on the Carlsberg bottle, post boxes, and Georg Jensen silverware. There are Royal Copenhagen designs for china which go back to the 18th century. Denmark, however, is no sterile design museum and there is constant renewal: you have only to think of the style and skills involved in producing the best-known consumer goods, such as CD players and televisions by Bang & Olufsen who introduced the concept of industrial design to home electronics.

Danish architects have been responsible for beautiful

modern buildings all over the world, most strikingly the Sydney Opera House by Jørn Utzon, and others are busy helping to rebuild Berlin. All round Denmark, too, there are well-designed public buildings – concert halls, railway stations, libraries and town halls.

Unfortunately, design skills are less frequently applied to domestic architecture and Denmark has its share of dreary blocks of flats and rows of ugly bungalows. Local and central government take so much tax to pay for the fine public buildings that there is little left for the taxpayers' own houses. There is no guarantee however that, left to themselves, taxpayers would buy better domestic architecture. Being born Danish does not guarantee impeccable taste.

Radio and Television

Danish radio stations are very good. D.R. (Danmarks Radio) the state station, is an institution and active in supporting young musicians and groups. By contrast, Danish television is widely regarded as being unimaginative and old-fashioned, so many people have turned to cable television as an alternative source of entertainment.

Even those television sets not specially hooked up can receive Swedish programmes in the east of the country and German programmes in the south. This has an effect on the language skills and cultural orientation of the different regions. People in the east understand Swedish; whereas southern Jutlanders speak excellent German having being brought up on a diet of foreign films dubbed in German – 'Ich heisse Bond, James Bond.'

Judging by programming schedules, Danes enjoy live audience debates. The same subjects are bandied about week after week (tax, immigrants, TV violence, welfare), starting at the same starting point and finishing in midsentence without reaching a specific outcome.

American films are popular and are subtitled, which means that when Danes drop, lose or break anything, they swear in English four-letter words. Cartoons with English soundtracks also draw large audiences. Those for younger children are dubbed. Older children must try and keep up with the subtitles. This can be difficult when you still haven't cracked the ABC code at the age of six.

Literature

No child in the world has not been affected by the tales of Hans Christian Andersen. This strange, shy man with his morally correct fairy stories put Denmark on the literary map and his fame contributes to huge sums spent by tourists. The sculpture of his Little Mermaid is the only landmark for which Denmark is famous.

The Danes are conscious of their national icon being a modest affair – a life-size mermaid sitting on a little rock, forever gazing out to sea. Yet the setting of the statue, windswept and lonely, is strangely dramatic. The family of the original sculptor make a handsome living from sales of Little Mermaid merchandise. Everything, from postcards to scale models cast in bronze, has to be approved by them.

Apart from Hans Christian Andersen, whose thinking is easy to understand but whose writing is inelegant, the most famous Danish writer is Søren Kierkegaard, whose writing is elegant but whose thinking is difficult to understand. Kierkegaard is credited with (or blamed for) being the founder of existentialism; in his lifetime hardly anyone read his works, and those who did thought he was a nuisance. Nevertheless he has had an influence far beyond the borders of Denmark.

Of two Danes who shared a Nobel prize for literature – Pontoppidan and Gjellerup – not much is heard outside Denmark which is a pity, in particular in the case of

Pontoppidan who wrote novels dealing with the struggle between man's ambition and his being true to his essential self.

The character of Danish culture springs from the relationship of the Danes to their natural surroundings. Culture for them is a way of shedding the modern world and getting back to their roots. All Danes are inveterate nature lovers. They cultivate an almost masochistic feeling of insignificance coupled with awe at nature's power and the forces of life. Danish literature is full of examples of characters trying to come to terms with man's essential loneliness and unimportance.

Tom Kristensen's 1930 classic *Hærværk* (*Havoc*), is the story of a once politically active journalist who deliberately sets out to destroy himself and his new respectable life through drink and infidelity.

In Pontoppidan's greatest work, *Lykke Per*, the hero is a priest's son from a country district, who has great belief in himself and unrealistic ambition, yet he is given the chance to realise his ambition and achieve greatness. Just when success and happiness are in his grasp he turns his back on them and embraces failure and unhappiness, because he realises that this is what fate ordained for him; this is how he must be true to his innermost self. It is as if Pontoppidan turns the story of the Ugly Duckling on its head; if you are born a duck you can dream about being a swan, but you are still a duck.

Karen Blixen was less philosophically motivated in her writing, though she is nevertheless seen as a feminist heroine because of her struggle to overcome the affliction of a wastrel husband who spent her money and infected her with syphilis before abandoning her. Confusingly, she wrote under the various names of Karen Blixen, Isak Dinesen and Pierre Andrézel. But now she is to be eternally remembered as Meryl Streep in *Out of Africa*.

A modern star in the literary firmament is Peter Høeg, who has overcome the difficulty of having such a surname to hit the big time with *Miss Smilla's Feeling for Snow*, a murder mystery which interweaves closely observed details of everyday Danish life with philosophical musings and sheer fantasy.

The Performing Arts

The nation competes in the première league in the world of ballet. The Royal Danish Ballet is famous for being the home of the 19th-century choreographer, August Bournonville, whose ballets include the immortal *La Sylphide*.

The oldest film company in the world, Nordisk Films, (founded in 1905) is Danish. A pair of Danish film comedians called Lighthouse and Trailer (on account of one being tall and thin and the other being short and round) were world famous until the talkies came along.

Working against the disadvantage of having only a small market for films in their own language, Danish film makers have nevertheless had international success with Bille August's *Pelle the Conqueror* and *Smilla's Feeling for Snow*, Lars von Trier's *Europa* and *Breaking the Waves*, Gabriel Axel's *Babette's Feast*, and *Festen* by Thomas Vinterberg.

The name of Carl Th. Dreyer is known to a growing circle of film aficionados. He produced films which were full of doom and symbolism, and, working in the medium of black and white, was particularly skilful in his use of the black. Recently, a peculiarly Danish school of film called *dogme* has emerged that supports a kind of relaxed, natural hand-held filming realism. However the strict rules for filming are anything but relaxed.

A unique form of entertainment is the *revy* (revue). In the summer, professional and amateur actors, singers and entertainers in all provincial towns put on entertainments that are local, topical, amusing and musical. The audience delights in having things said and sung about their own community, and local dignitaries are treated with anything but dignity. It is a bit like pantomime except that the jokes, like the Dame's padded attributes, are well over the heads of any children present.

The great figure of Danish music is Carl Nielsen. Born into a poor family on the island of Funen, his father supplemented the family income by going out and playing folk music. Unlike his contemporary, Sibelius, whose works express and embody the Finnish national spirit, Nielsen's symphonies are distinctive but not nationalistic; they have a vigour which is strangely at odds with the Danes' equable temperament and the quiet Danish landscape.

He also wrote many songs, and set Danish poems to music. These are lyrical and tuneful, often expressing a love of the countryside, and have become part of the national heritage. *The Danish Song*, a Neilsen composition for a poem by Kai Hoffmann (first performed in 1926), echoes these sentiments:

> The Danish song is a young blonde girl who is humming
>   in Denmark's house.
> She is the child of the sea-blue kingdom, where beech
>   trees listen to the froth of the waves.

Painters

At the turn of the 20th century, the town of Skagen on the northern tip of Jutland was home to a school of painters. Its clear skies, and pale gold and platinum sands inspired artists like P.S. Krøyer, Michael and Anna Ancher, L.A. Ring, and others not necessarily working in Skagen, like Hammershøi and J.F. Willumsen, who developed a technique for showing how light plays on water and in the air. Constantly reproduced on greetings cards, their images of seashores and sunlight, family parties, domestic interiors, fishermen and country workers are invested with dignity enriched by affection. In rather the same way as some 17th-century Dutch painters celebrated their everyday life, they made the ordinary look beautiful, and full-length petticoats remain whiter than white, even after long strolls along the shore.

Systems

Getting About

Things work in Denmark. They work without a great bureaucratic superstructure and without bribery or obligatory tips. Taxis have notices saying a service charge is included in the price – though *drikkepenge* (drinking money) is accepted with a smile.

You can set your watch by the local suburban trains. Buses also run on time, and there are plenty of them. Motorways take you almost wherever you want to go. (You may not realise you have arrived, however, because the names on street signs are so small, they are hard to read from a moving vehicle.)

The excellence of the transport system owes much to the fact that, as there are no motor car factories in the country, the transport policy has been framed according to the needs of the users, and not to the need to protect jobs. It has allowed the development of efficient public transport, saving Denmark from an excess of motorways, traffic jams and commuter stress. A bonus is that it reduces the need for parking facilities, promotes communal feeling, and helps the environment.

With no domestic car production, the Danes are able to put a high tax on the purchase of motor vehicles without this being regarded as a protective tariff or damaging to Danish industry. On the contrary, the policy promotes employment because one in three vehicles on the road in Denmark is over ten years old, skilfully kept going by the car servicing sector. It also keeps the bicycle trade riding high.

Hundreds of thousands of people use bicycles as a primary means of getting about. Copenhagen operates a clever scheme which imitates the coin-in-the-slot trolley system. From a stand of sponsored bicycles provided by the council you can disconnect one, cycle around town, and retrieve your coin when you put back the bike in another stand.

Motorists give way to cyclists, cyclists give way to pedestrians, and pedestrians give way to traffic lights. Rollerblade users give way to no-one.

With over 60 domestic ferry routes linking the islands, all Danish families use them at one time or another. One of the pleasures of travelling to and fro has always been the opportunity to get out of the car or off the train and stretch your legs, breathe fresh air, enjoy a snack, see who else may be on board, and generally slow down and relax.

The 60 minute ferry ride steaming across the Storebælt (Great Belt) between Zealand and Funen, has now been replaced by the longest suspension bridge in Europe. After 10 years of financial difficulties, engineering problems and political wrangling, this magnificent 4-mile bridge-tunnel link has at last been completed. It now takes travellers only 10 minutes to cross, but another 50 minutes waiting in a queue to buy a ticket.

The bridge to Sweden is another new landmark. To avoid problems with low flying aircraft at Copenhagen Airport, designers created a tunnel that leads to an artificial island where the bridge begins.

The bridge is named the Øresundsbron, a word that is half Danish and half Swedish. The Danes aren't really bothered about what it's called. What self-respecting Dane would want to go to Sweden anyway?

Education and Training

The Danes believe they have the highest educational standards in the world. This belief is based on the traditional length of university degree courses, and the thoroughness of vocational training.

School starts at the age of six, before which children are not encouraged to read or write (the attitude is: let kids play while they are young). As a result, and because many letters in the Danish alphabet are 'dual-action' or silent in spoken Danish, spelling is not a Danish forte. The Danes find this difficult to swallow, along with their glottal stops.

At about the age of 16 the more practically talented receive vocational training, and the more academically minded move up to a *gymnasium* (high school), and from there to university. Until recently the average time taken to get a first degree was roughly ten years. This was because the minimum standard time was about six years, so students had to get jobs to support themselves while they studied, and so took longer to complete the course. Because they took longer to complete the course they would start having families so they took longer still to complete the course. Even so, it has always taken a very long time to get a university degree – though Danes like to relate this to the depth of study rather than any slowness of progress.

Shops and Shopping

Danish commerce has the concept of 'loyal competition'. Everyone has a living to make, and in the long run people will be losers if they try to take the bread out of someone else's mouth. A consequence of all this consensus is that the monopolies commission is kept busy and prices remain high. Not that it matters because you can get a reasonable price for whatever you buy when you sell it again in *Den Blå Avis* (The Blue Paper). This nationwide, now electronic newspaper, offers everything second-hand that you can imagine – furniture, tractors, horses, cars, clothes, even maternity bras, and needless to say scores of bikes are 'recycled' every week.

Because the Danes believe in quality more than convenience, there are still many independent specialist shopkeepers. In an effort to compete with the superstores, they do what they're good at: they form an organisation, design a good logo, brainstorm a slogan (e.g., 'Covers everything' for an indoor shopping centre, or 'Best in the long run' for a bumpy old high street which is more expensive on shoe leather), and then co-operate in groups to share costs of purchasing and marketing. As a result, not every Danish high street looks like every other high street.

In addition to supermarkets there are hypermarkets which are occupation based, for example one for teachers and another for caterers. There are also two types of chemist – the *apoteket* and the *materialist*. The *apoteket* is really a pharmacist concentrating mostly on selling medicines. The *materialist* sells goods which, in Britain, would be spread between the chemist, the ironmonger, the garden centre and the pet shop. Here you can find alternative medicines, flea powder, fertiliser, loofahs, soap, shampoo, face flannels, turpentine, charcoal for the barbecue and jars of *kopatte salve* (cow udder ointment) as a remedy for chapped hands.

The difference in the cost of living between Denmark and Germany, especially in luxury products like spirits and tobacco, tempts many Danes to chance the attentions of Customs and Excise. Border trade is worth millions of pounds a year and although E.U. regulations are evening out the differences, Danes still flock to the special supermarkets built for their custom that throng the German border area in south Jutland.

Smuggling is also a pensioner sport, with all sorts of

cunning tricks being practised. One favourite is taking a thermos of coffee on the trip, drinking the coffee on the ferry and filling the thermos up with spirits on the way back. Five minutes before arriving in the Danish port, the lavatories on board are occupied by pensioners stuffing cigarettes down their trousers and decanting whisky into more innocent-looking containers. An elderly couple were fined for having smuggled a total of 800 litres of spirits and 30,000 cigarettes into Denmark. They claimed in court that these were for private use because they were saving up for the husband's 80th birthday party.

Crime and Punishment

Except when outwitting the taxman, the Danes are a law-abiding people. Like law-abiding people everywhere, motorists break the speed limit. At zebra crossings they only stop for really assertive pedestrians, who are more inclined to wave them on in case they get mown down. This is why Danes show remarkable obedience as pedestrians at controlled crossings, submitting their free will to the little red man, and standing forever on the kerb of an empty street until he gives way to the green.

As a nation within Europe, Denmark (together with Britain) tops the list of countries which most dutifully enact domestic legislation to implement European laws.

There is no generalised regime of violence, no street where it is unsafe to walk. From time to time there are confrontations between the police and politically motivated groups, like squatters or strikers, but if this results in violence a sense of shock ripples throughout the country that any Danes should resort to such methods.

Imprisonment in Denmark is not intended to brutalise the prisoner. The theory is that if you treat him brutally, he will behave brutally. So most prisoners are able to have some form of normal life while serving their sentences, keeping in touch with their families, going home at weekends, even carrying on their businesses by telephone and correspondence. It may appear a soft option, but it's hard to fault as it seems to work.

Business and Commerce

The Guild System

The whole of Danish business life is marked by the residual spirit of the guild system. Vocational training is still required for most jobs. This applies not only to doctors, dentists and lawyers, but all kinds of trades.

In order to change an electric bulb, you must be a fully trained electric bulb changer. Your training as an electric bulb changer will be very thorough, including a review of the history of electric bulbs, and, of course, sockets; the variety of designs and purposes of electric bulbs will be considered, as well as their social role, and the possible consequences of poorly-fitted bulbs. Once you are a certified electric bulb changer, you will become a member of the electric bulb changers' union and get a job, or at the very least, become a member of that union's publicly funded unemployment scheme.

The guild system is reinforced by the way in which unemployment pay is administered. For instance, the Candlestick Makers' Union administers the unemployment fund for candlestick makers. A candlestick maker may not be obliged to join the union, but if he wants unemployment insurance, for which he has already largely paid through his taxes, he has to subscribe for it through the union's unemployment scheme.

This leads to inflexibility in the labour market. If a candlestick maker loses his job and seeks work as a broomstick maker, he must leave the candlestick maker's unemployment fund and put at risk his being able to get work again as a candlestick maker, despite his long years of training.

Thus the modern Dane suffers from the new feudalism, bound to his house by debt and to his trade by the unemployment and qualification schemes.

Service and Manufacturing

With no raw materials of their own, the Danes have become adept at carving themselves a niche in the international chain of production. Danish companies specialise in quality, research, efficiency, know-how and consultancy. These they 'implement' with a lot of team spirit and all the latest management techniques.

Amazingly for its size, Denmark has some very high-profile multinational companies: Bang & Olufsen, of course, Carlsberg, LEGO (still massive after all these years of electronic toys), Mærsk, the oil, shipping and transport giant, and Novo Nordisk, a powerful chemical concern specialising in medicine and gene-spliced products. The Danes' strong point seems to be to offer high-quality products that others want to buy.

They have managed to grab a sizeable piece of the action in some unexpected areas, like marine electronics and insulin (which is linked to pig farming), pipeline assembly and container storage facilities. The biggest industrial sector is agriculture together with associated food-processing industries like bacon, butter and beer. The leading manufacturer of potato crisps is also the leading distiller of *snaps*, both being the product of the humble spud. Farming may now be capital intensive but the autumn school half-term is still referred to as the 'potato holiday', from the days when children were wanted in the fields to bring in the harvest.

The most characteristic Danish workplace is small, run by highly trained, self-employed people making products such as chocolate manufacturing machinery, pumps and compressors, furniture, boats, porcelain, and furs.

A high proportion of the Danish workforce is employed in the service sector. Quite apart from the usual service industries, like banks, transport, utilities, etc., this sector is swollen by the number of carers employed. Mr. Hansen goes out to work to look after Mrs. Jensen's mother in an old people's daycare centre. To be able to go out to work, Mr. Hansen has to leave his children in a daycare centre. Mrs. Jensen takes her mother to the old people's daycare centre on her way to work, which consists of looking after Mr. Hansen's children at the children's care centre.

In the Office

In many fields, being smart is a state of mind, not of clothing. Wearing a suit to the office is rarely required unless executives from a foreign parent company are likely to drop in. Feeling comfortable and at ease is all part of creating a good atmosphere in which to conduct a productive meeting. This overt friendliness can be misunderstood. Danes don't exactly roll up their sleeves and kick off their shoes, but they seem to be quick to get their feet under the table. They mix business and pleasure, sometimes telling jokes to break the ice, or beginning the agenda by offering beers all round at 10 o'clock in the morning.

There are no long business lunches; with flexi-time, lunch hours are often lunch half-hours. Middle managers shuffle along the canteen queue with everyone else or sit in the lunch room enjoying their *madpakke* (packed lunch) and a lager or *Danskvand* (Danish mineral water). Anything with *dansk* in its name has to be good.

Competitors are often acquaintances, for in a small country like Denmark it is likely that one manager has been at business school with another, or that they have been colleagues, or can expect to become so. Bosses will listen to the views of people lower down the hierarchical ladder because they believe them to be knowledgeable about their own sphere.

Nobody gets to the corporate starting posts without an excellent exam result and preferably some form of relevant work experience, be it only low-level work in the summer holidays while studying.

Danish employers demand a great deal from their employees but they also respect them and treat them accordingly. Promotion is performance-based and the workload is extreme. Big firms with multinational clients are expected to be on call 24 hours a day, which means that if the phone rings from Hong Kong at 3.30 in the morning you jump out of bed, drive to the office and get cracking.

Government

The Queen

Denmark is a constitutional monarchy – one of those which are sometimes disparagingly described as a 'bicycle monarchy'. There is, however, nothing of the freewheeler about the Danish Queen.

Margrethe, known affectionately as Daisy, is looked up to not just because she is tall, but because she is multi-talented. In addition to costume design for television theatre and scenery for ballet, she is an accomplished linguist and artist: the Danish publication of Simone de Beauvoir's *All Humans are Mortal* is her translation and her illustrations grace a special edition of *The Lord of The Rings*. She has also designed commemorative postage stamps, and created needlework patterns which anyone can buy and sew. Her only self-confessed failing is that she smokes, for which the populace love her even more.

Rain or shine, on her birthday hordes of flag-waving Danes congregate beneath her bedroom window to shout "Queen, Queen come out! Or we won't go home!" – and she does, despite the absence of the word 'please'.

Political Parties

The Danish voter has a plethora of political parties to choose from since any party getting 2% or more of the popular vote is assured parliamentary representation.

There are so many parties in Parliament (*Folketing*) that no party can ever rule without the support of others, and no party is ever without hope of having a share of government. The Government is therefore always a coalition government and sometimes, even as a coalition, it can still run the country with a minority in Parliament. This means that no politician can ever be too rude about another politician, whatever his views, because he never knows when he will need the other's support. Co-operation and self-interest are close cousins.

It requires a certain dedication to follow the differences in policies and personalities, or even to understand which party stands where on the political spectrum. *Venstre* ('Left'), the Liberals, is a party of the right, while *Venstre-socialisterne* (Left Socialists) are to the left of the Social Democrats, which puts the latter somewhere near the centre. The Central Democrats are to the right of centre, and *Radikale Venstre* (Radical Left) is neither radical nor left, but so far to the middle it is said that their standard response to political proposals from other parties is: "We're neither for nor against. On the contrary!"

In fact, all governments more or less pursue a Social Democratic policy, whichever party is in office. An ex prime minister once said that the trouble with the Danes is that they "Work black, eat green and vote red".

The Green Party has made little headway in Denmark

which may seem strange in a country so concerned with the environment. But the fact is that there is such a broad consensus on environmental issues across the political spectrum, there has been no need for people to support the Green Party in order to get mainstream issues addressed.

Denmark does have a right-wing political party. It was started in 1972 by a tax lawyer, Mogens Glistrup, to protest against high taxes. Glistrup is about as close as Denmark gets to having an eccentric. During the height of the Cold War, he suggested getting rid of the Danish army, navy and air force and substituting a telephone at the border linked to an answering machine carrying the message "We surrender, we surrender".

Glistrup himself had to withdraw from active politics for a while when the courts took a dimmer view of his tax affairs than the electorate did. Every now and then, he finds his way back into polite political circles, disgraces himself publicly and is banished once more, in the manner of a bloodhound on an over-rich diet.

A professional comedian called Jacob Haugaard was voted into parliament with his one-man Party for Work-Shy Elements. One of his election promises was to provide a following wind on cycle paths.

Language

Danish is not a beautiful language. But it is economical. Why invent a new word when two old ones are perfectly adequate? For example, direct translations give: the dust sucker (vacuum cleaner), swine meat (pork), beating meat (stewing beef), body burning (cremation), flying machine (aeroplane) and breast wart (nipple). Words, like everything else, are recycled where possible: *hej* means hello, *hej, hej* means goodbye. The verb *at lide* can mean to suffer or to like. *Fyr* means fire, pine or young man. *Brud* means rupture, bride or weasel. Listeners have to pay attention to context and tone of voice if misunderstandings are to be avoided. Perhaps this is why Denmark produces about 25% of the world's hearing aids.

Danes, Norwegians and Swedes are tuned to each other's languages and can converse in their native tongues, though Danish and Norwegian sound very different. It has been observed that people in hilly countries speak with up-and-down sing-song accents. People in flat countries speak with flat accents. Denmark is a flat country.

There is no system of phonetic notation that can do justice to spoken Danish. The consonants are often so softly enunciated as to be undetectable except to the trained ear, while the language possesses vowels which require the speaker to make noises that would be inadmissible in polite society in any other civilised country.

Then there's the 'r'. The Italians and Scots roll their r's at the tip of their tongues; the German guttural 'r' is pronounced from the back of the throat. The Danish 'r' has to be fetched from deep below the tonsils, and requires special muscles.

A knowledge of the Danish alphabet may seem esoteric, but it can be helpful to know that, in looking up words in a dictionary, names in a telephone directory or places in a street map, v and w may be treated as being the same, aa is the same as å, and æ, ø and å are at the end of the alphabet. Anyone looking for Aabenraa at the start of a list will look in vain.

One unequivocally positive thing can be said about the Danes and their language: though by mid-sentence they may begin to glance at their watches, they are endlessly tolerant of those who try to speak it. Maybe they recognise that Danish is so unspeakably difficult, no foreigner can make it worse.

The Authors

Helen Dyrbye (née Pearce) grew up on the east coast of England and learnt to sail on the Norfolk Broads. A career as P.R. assistant for the Scout Association was diverted by marriage to a Danish thatcher, and relocation to Denmark.

After two years of glottal stopping and starting, she began running English courses for business professionals. A published author of children's books, she also works as a language consultant and makes dreadful packed lunches. She dreams of finding a tax loophole big enough to buy a boat and teach her sons to sail.

Steven Harris was working for a multi-national in Brussels when he was moved to Copenhagen for 12 months' 'rotational' training. He went on rotating in Denmark for ten years. He knew he had mastered Danish when people stopped telling him how well he spoke it.

He now lives in England with his Danish wife and three children, and works from home as an intellectual odd-job man – translating Danish into English and doing market consultancy in the legal and publishing worlds.

Thomas Golzen was born and brought up in London. He went to Denmark to work as a professional musician for three months in 1987, and never left.

After much travelling and a bewildering array of emergency jobs he settled in Copenhagen, where he still lives with his Danish partner and their two children. A graduate from the National Danish Film School, he is a freelance screenwriter. He also enjoys earning an extra bob or two by twanging his guitar, and helping to run emergency shelters for the Danish Red Cross.

Further titles in the Xenophobe's® Guide series
www.xenophobes.com